THE MINOANS AND THE MYCENAEANS

Greece Ancient History 5th Grade Children's Ancient History

Speedy Publishing LLC

40 E. Main St. #1156

Newark, DE 19711

www.speedypublishing.com

Copyright 2017

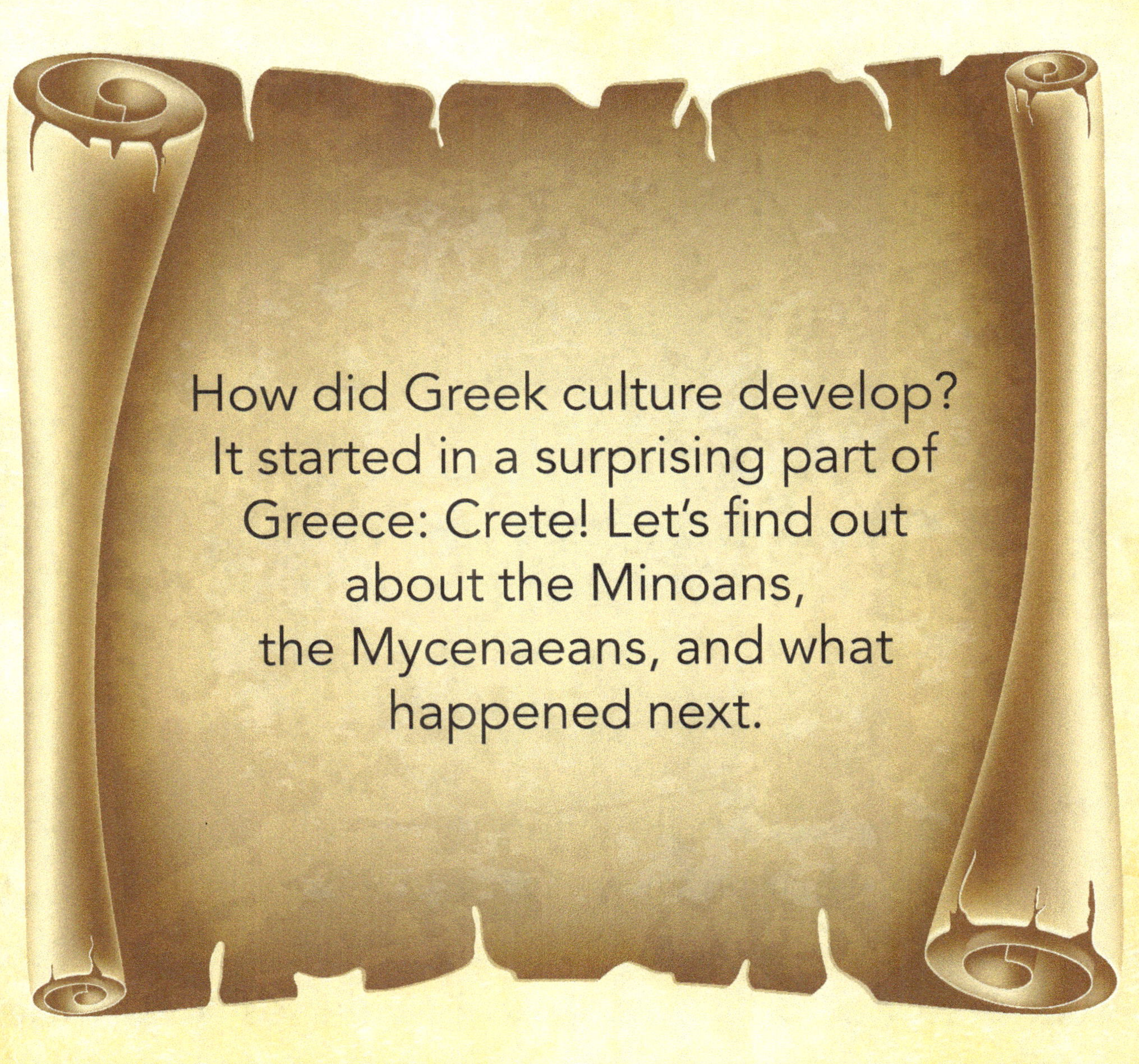

How did Greek culture develop?
It started in a surprising part of
Greece: Crete! Let's find out
about the Minoans,
the Mycenaeans, and what
happened next.

EARLY GREECE

There were people living in what is now Greece in prehistoric times. We know very little about these people, whom we call the Pelasgians. They used stone tools and lived in villages, not large cities.

SCENIC RUINS OF THE MINOAN PALACE

But it is not from them that the Greek culture we know of in myths, art, and literature like The Iliad comes from. The development of a rich culture, with writing, art, and history, comes first to Greece on the island of Crete, with the Minoans.

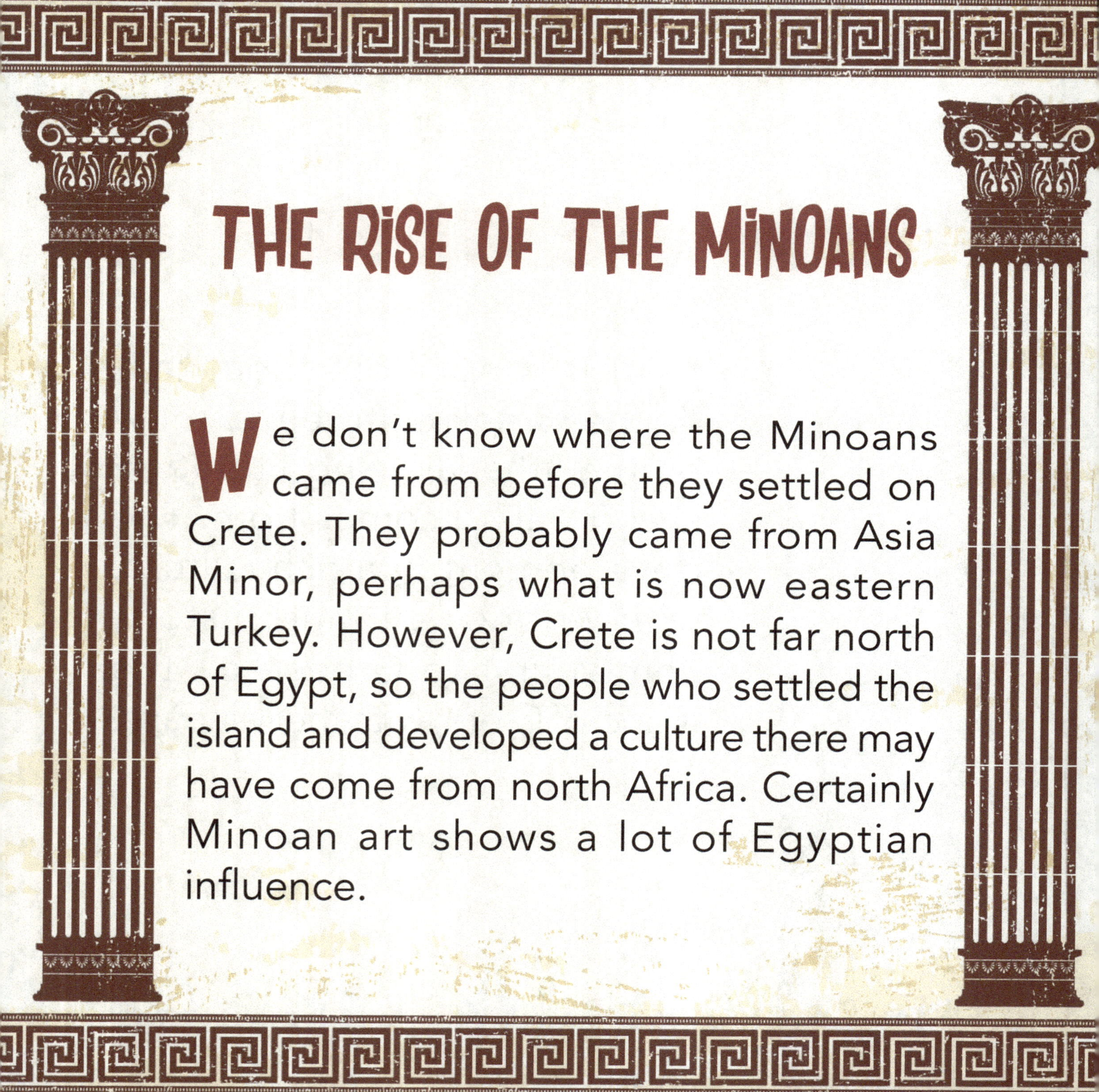

THE RISE OF THE MINOANS

We don't know where the Minoans came from before they settled on Crete. They probably came from Asia Minor, perhaps what is now eastern Turkey. However, Crete is not far north of Egypt, so the people who settled the island and developed a culture there may have come from north Africa. Certainly Minoan art shows a lot of Egyptian influence.

THE MINOAN CIVILIZATION OF CRETE

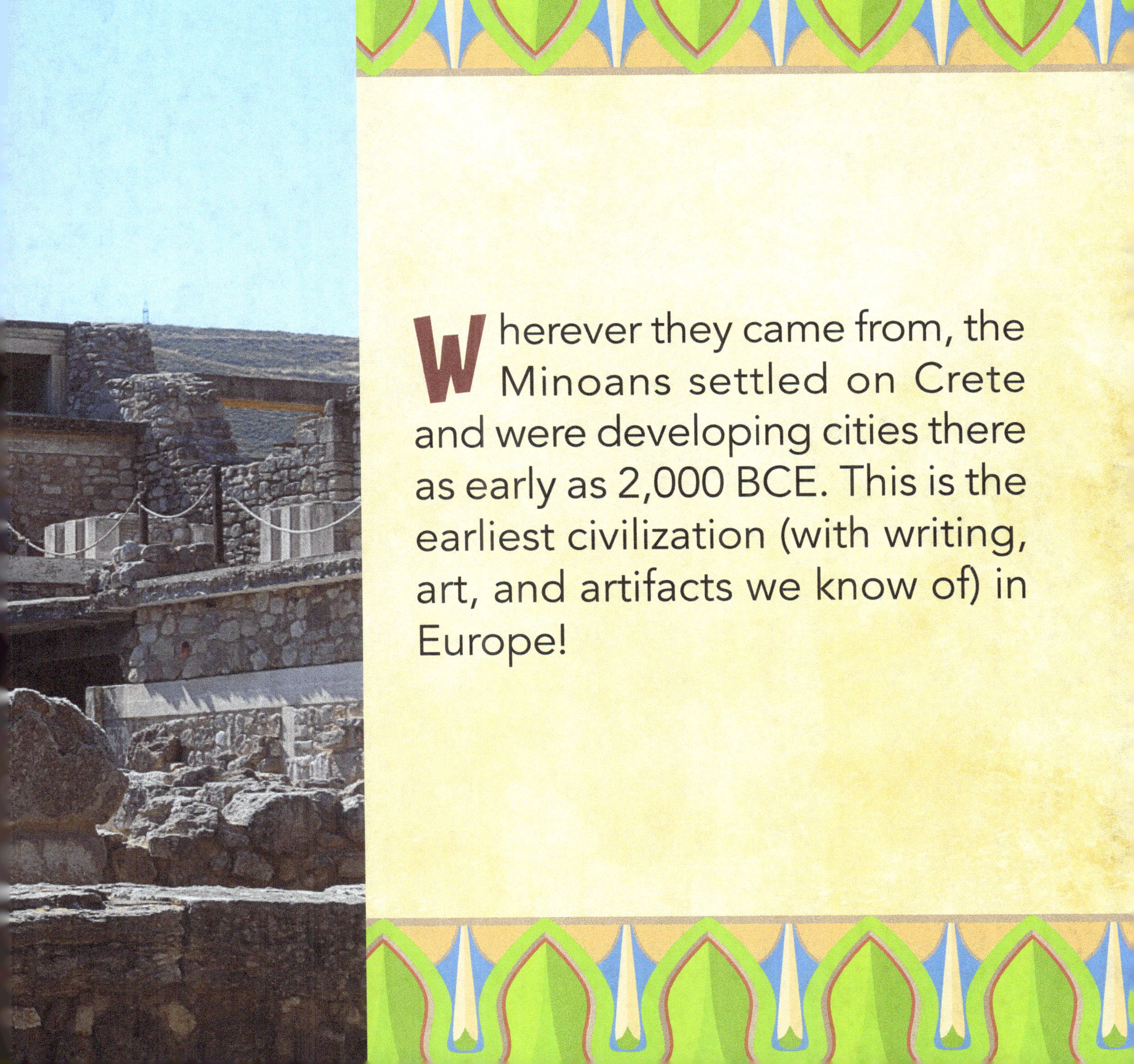

Wherever they came from, the Minoans settled on Crete and were developing cities there as early as 2,000 BCE. This is the earliest civilization (with writing, art, and artifacts we know of) in Europe!

Crete has a mild climate and fertile soil. This made it possible to support a growing population, and to create a wealthy culture. However, over time, the Minoans reached the limits of what the island could support. To continue to develop and grow, they had to locate more resources.

AGRICULTURE FIELDS

The Minoans made use of the position of Crete in the Mediterranean to become a trading nation. They bought and sold goods from other lands, generating wealth for themselves. Minoan ships seem to have been "armed freighters": they could carry a cargo of goods, but they also had a big enough crew and the right weapons to fight off attacks from other ships. Because the Minoan navy was so strong and so good at what it did, the Minoans did not spend much energy on putting walls around their cities.

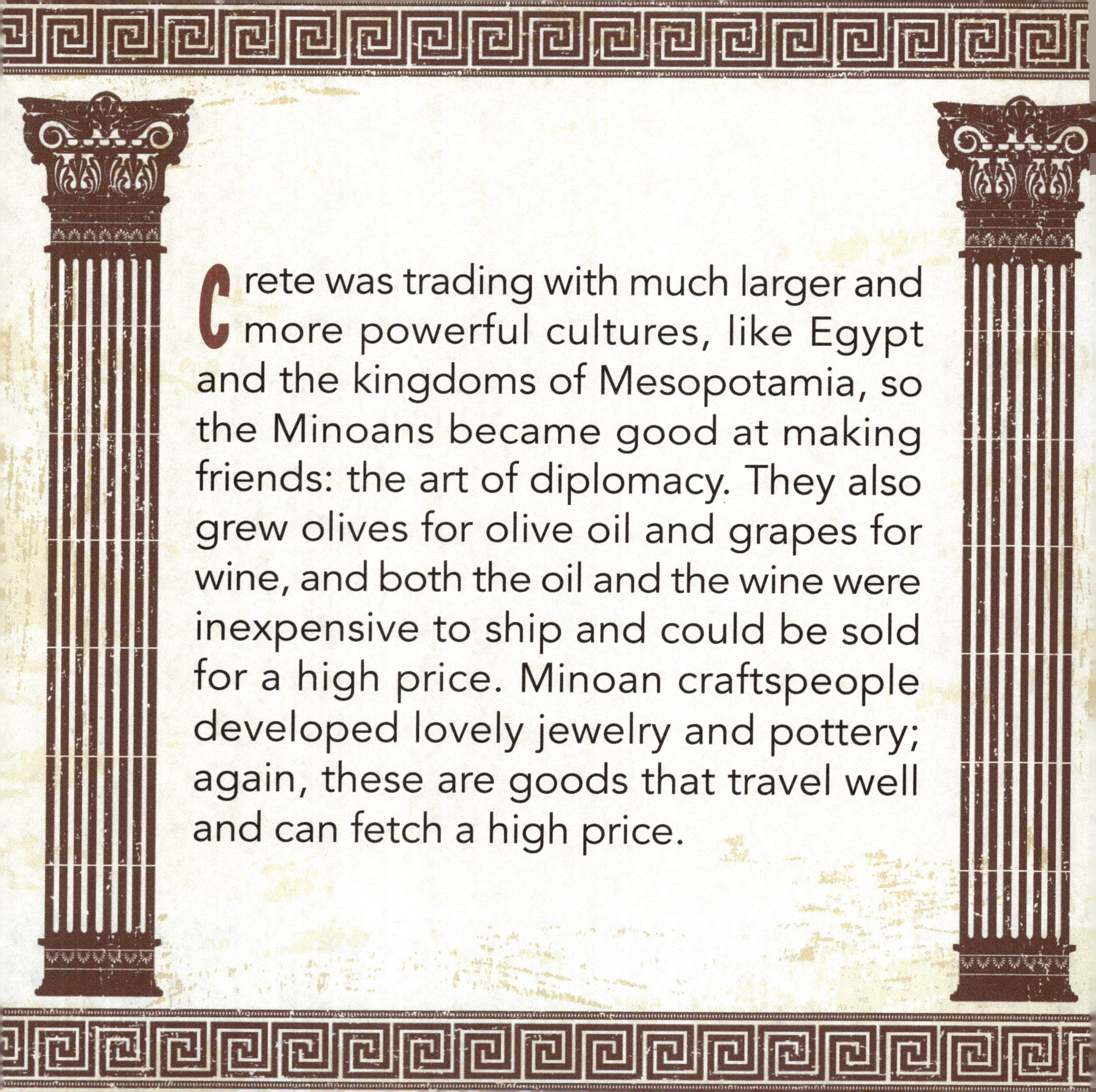

Crete was trading with much larger and more powerful cultures, like Egypt and the kingdoms of Mesopotamia, so the Minoans became good at making friends: the art of diplomacy. They also grew olives for olive oil and grapes for wine, and both the oil and the wine were inexpensive to ship and could be sold for a high price. Minoan craftspeople developed lovely jewelry and pottery; again, these are goods that travel well and can fetch a high price.

POTTERY AT THE ARCHAEOLOGICAL SITE OF KNOSSOS, CRETE

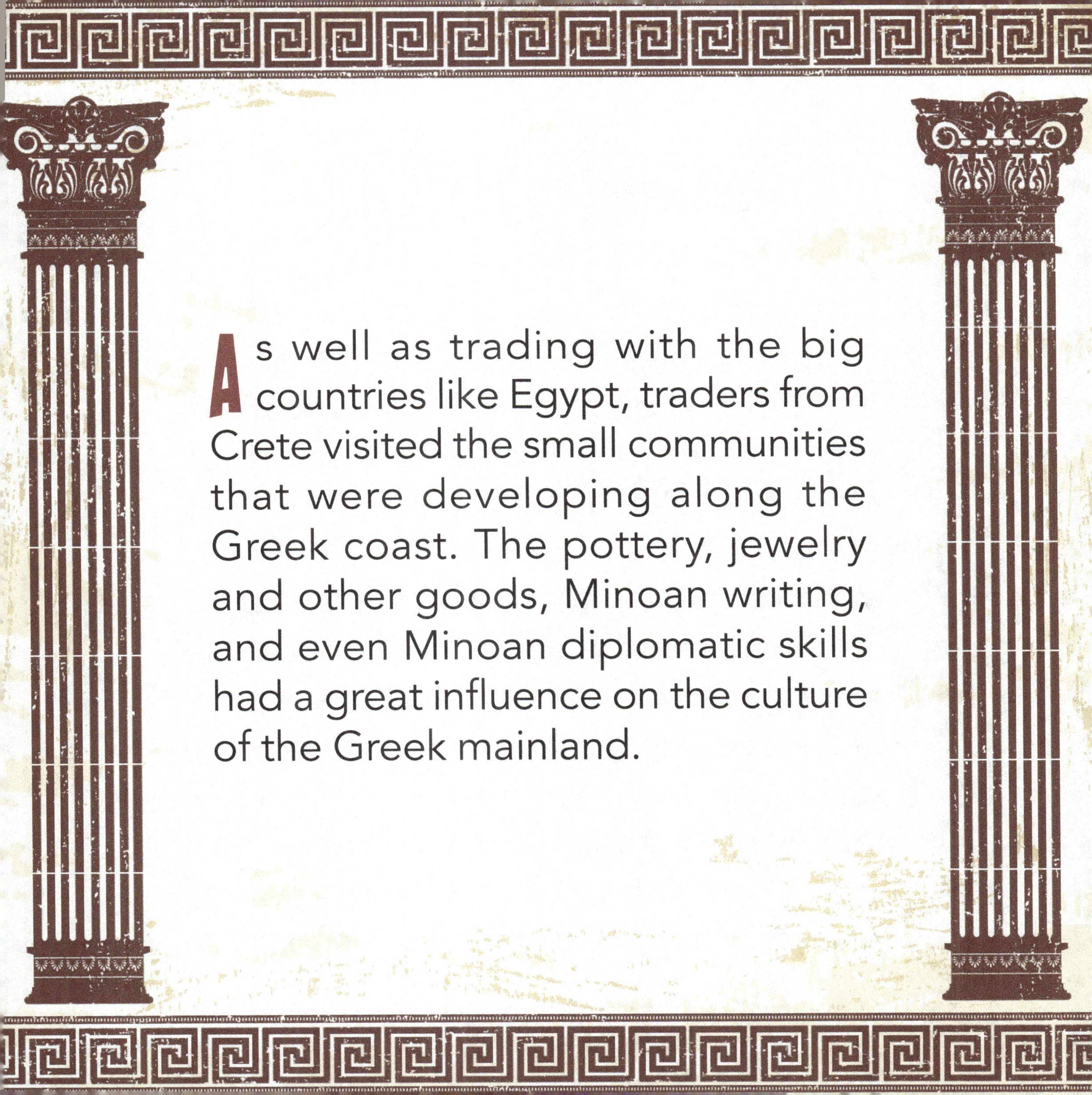

As well as trading with the big countries like Egypt, traders from Crete visited the small communities that were developing along the Greek coast. The pottery, jewelry and other goods, Minoan writing, and even Minoan diplomatic skills had a great influence on the culture of the Greek mainland.

MINOAN CULTURE

The Minoans probably learned writing from the Egyptians. Later, they adapted Egyptian writing into a more phonetic alphabet. We have found thousands of clay tablets and other material with Minoan writing, which we call Linear A, but it is very hard to figure out what the messages are about. Scholars believe most of the documents have to do with buying, selling, and shipping material. A society that lives by trading has to have a good way of keeping track of what it shipped, what it sold for, and where the money is!

ANCIENT INSCRIPTION ON A ROCK

MINOAN COLONY IN BAY

The Minoans were probably the most wealthy of all the early societies. They had a good income from trading, and spent very little of it on armies and fortifications because they had a good natural defense: the sea. There was probably a king and a class of noble families at the top, but everybody on Crete seems to have had enough. Even the poorest households seem to have lived in houses with many rooms.

Palaces in Crete were sprawling complexes with hundreds of rooms. The government probably had a lot of scribes, writing and reading all those tablets, and a lot of storage places for all the goods they bought and sold.

OLIVE OIL STORAGE CELLAR

i n later Greek myths, the people of Crete are shown as loving spectator sports like boxing and bull-jumping (the player grabs the horns of a charging bull and vaults over the bull's back). Women had a more active role in Minoan society than in many other early cultures. Wall paintings even show women bull-jumpers!

We know very little of Minoan religion. Most of the gods seem to have been female.

Minoan paintings and carvings were not about battles and rarely about their gods. Instead, the art of Crete was mainly to decorate homes and palaces with pleasant scenes. Because art did not record the actions of great kings or the results of great battles, we know very little of the history of Crete during the Minoan era.

OLD WALLS OF CRETE

RISE OF THE MYCENAEANS

The rich Minoan culture must have been a challenge and an inspiration to the people on the mainland of Greece. However, each small city on the mainland had to look to its defense at all times, as it had ambitious neighbors on all sides and no natural defenses besides some mountains. Greek city-states tended to develop with strong defensive walls and with armies that were expensive in resources and manpower.

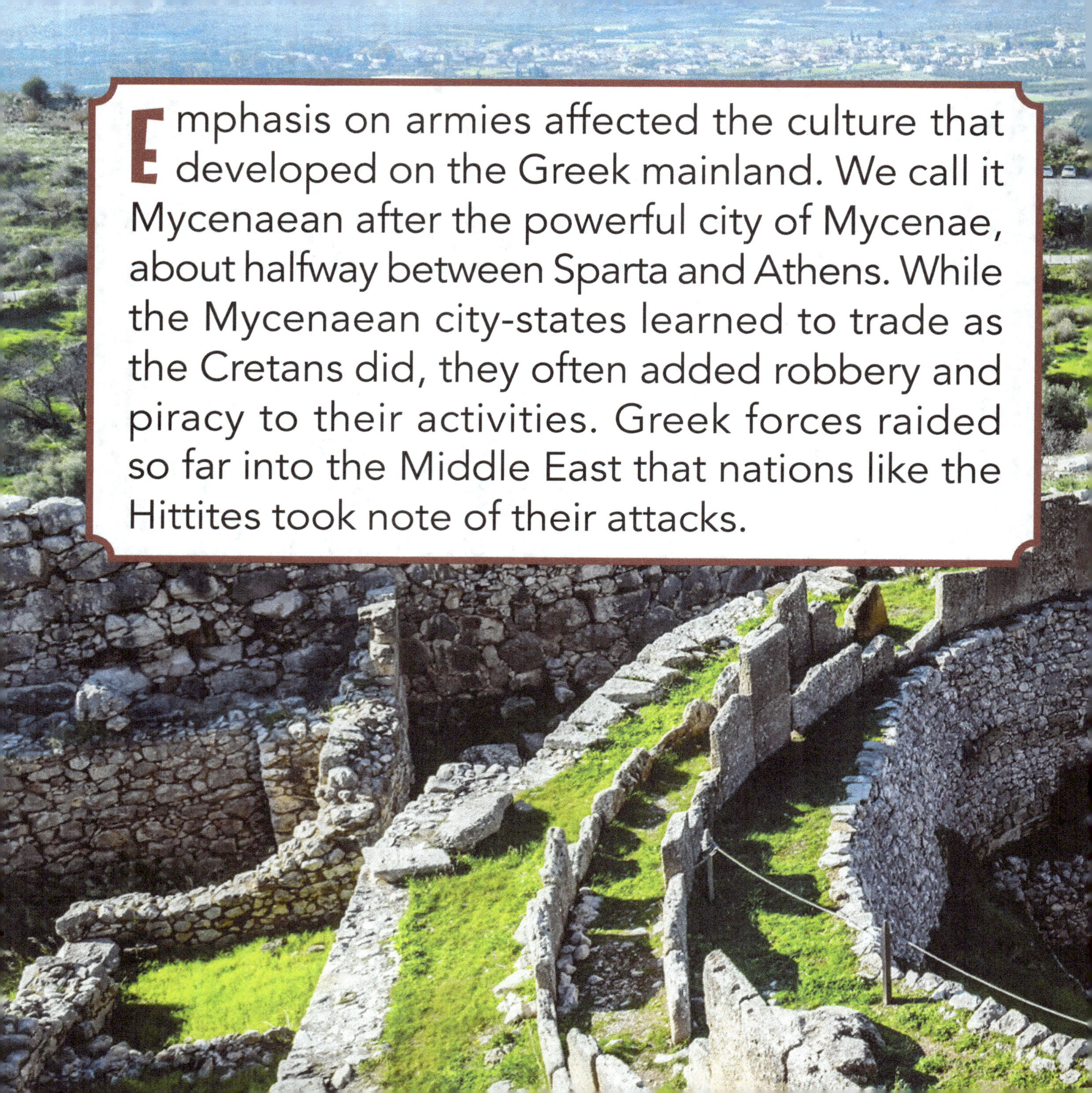

Emphasis on armies affected the culture that developed on the Greek mainland. We call it Mycenaean after the powerful city of Mycenae, about halfway between Sparta and Athens. While the Mycenaean city-states learned to trade as the Cretans did, they often added robbery and piracy to their activities. Greek forces raided so far into the Middle East that nations like the Hittites took note of their attacks.

MYCENAE, ARCHAEOLOGICAL PLACE AT GREECE

STATUE OF HOMER, ANCIENT GREEK POET

Mycenaean culture celebrated strength, warfare, and conquest in a way that the Minoan culture did not. The great stories of the Mycenaean period are adventures and tales of conquest, like the Iliad and the Odyssey, which the blind poet Homer arranged into dramatic form and sang for many audiences.

COMPARING THE TWO CULTURES

Both societies were more complex than a brief summary can cover, and evolved over the hundreds of years they existed. They interacted with each other and influenced each other.

COWS

owever, here are some characteristics that can help you remember the difference between Minoan and Mycenaean culture:

- Minoans had an economy based on the sea: fishing and trade. Mycenaeans were land-based: farming, cattle, horses, and battle.

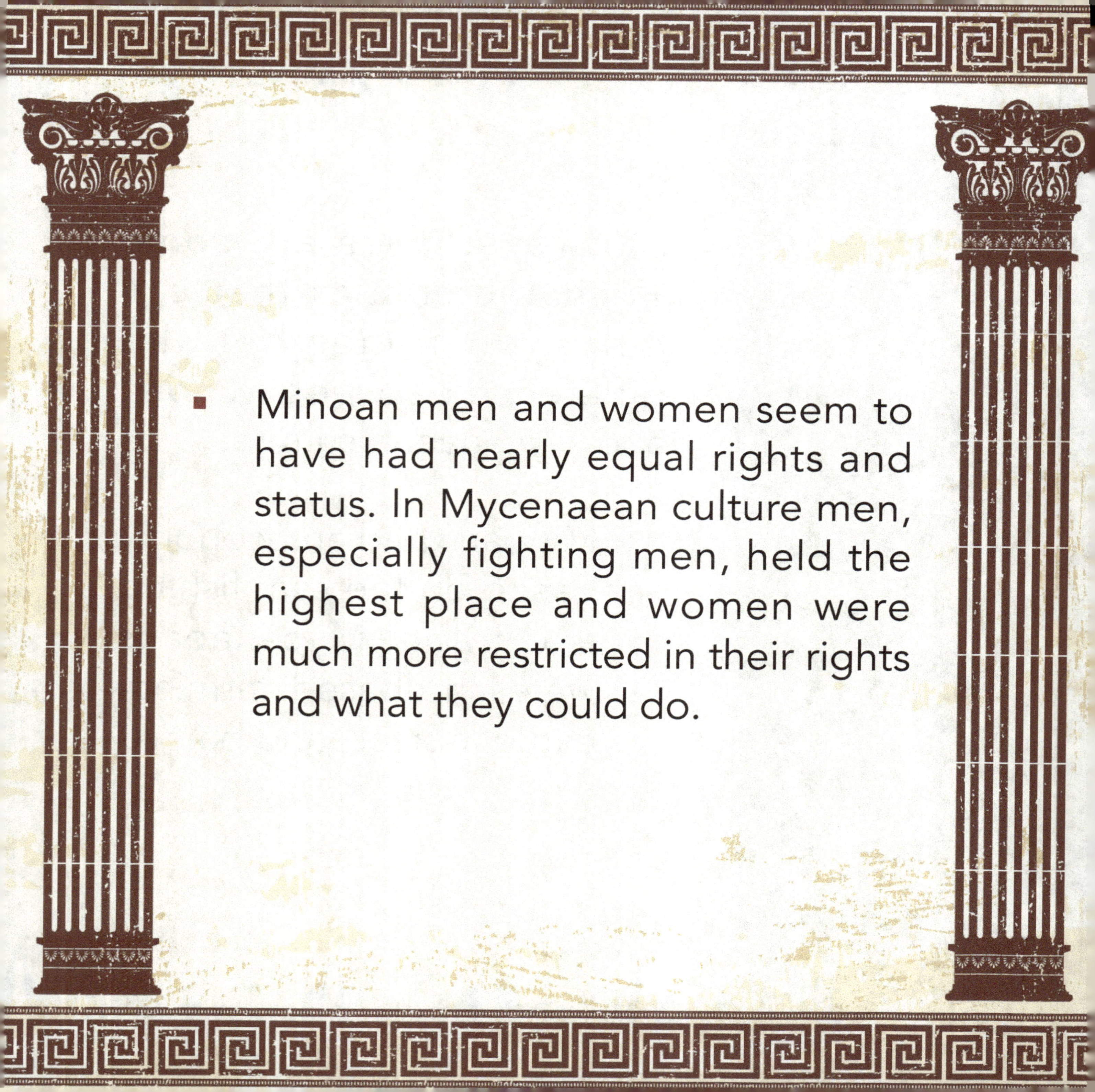

- Minoan men and women seem to have had nearly equal rights and status. In Mycenaean culture men, especially fighting men, held the highest place and women were much more restricted in their rights and what they could do.

ILLUSTRATION OF A ANCIENT MINOAN WOMAN

FiGHTERS

- Minoans relied heavily on negotiations, allies, treaties, and diplomacy to make trade possible. Mycenaean city-states relied more on military might, adventures, conquests, and brute force to gain riches and resources.

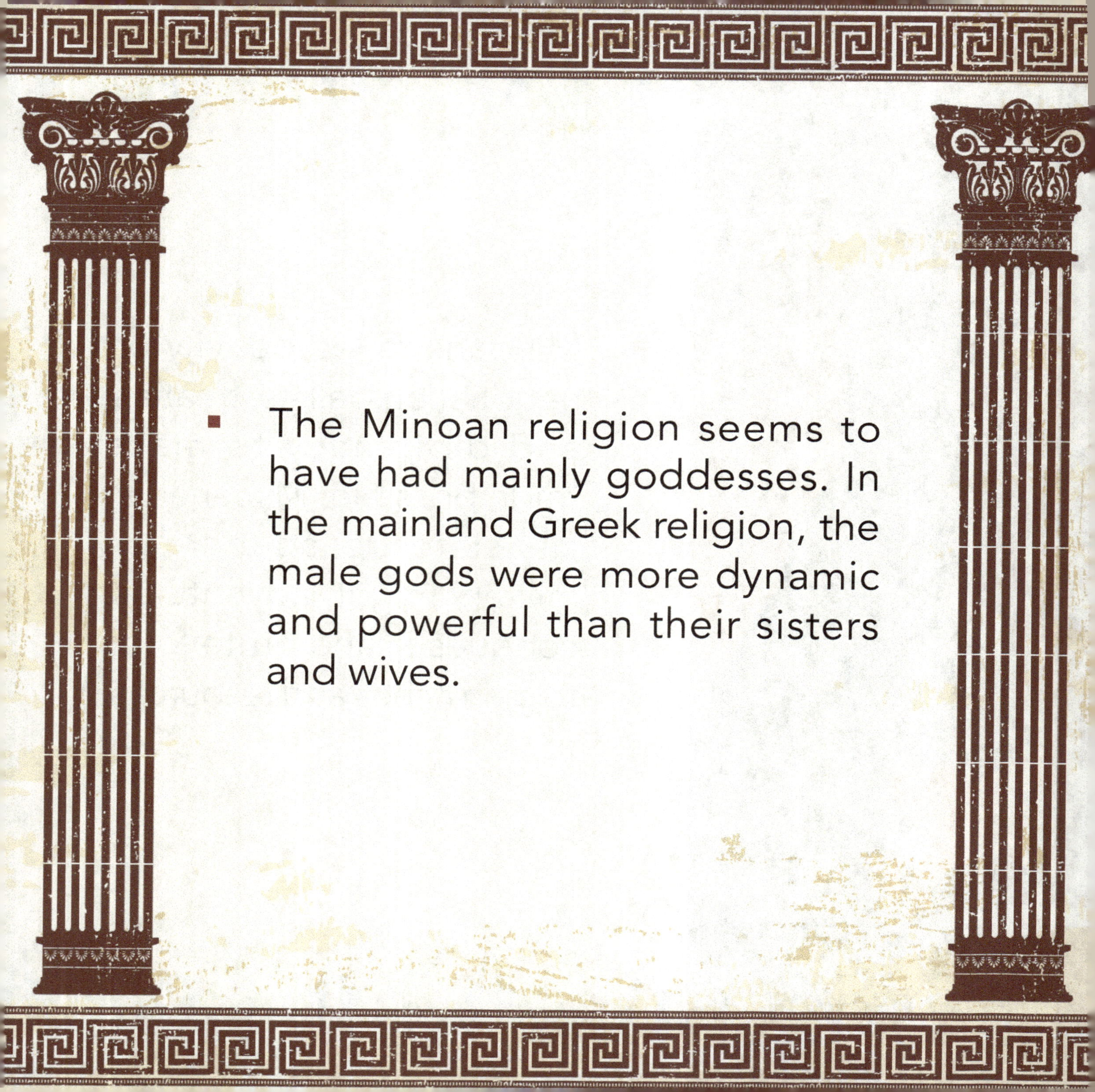

- The Minoan religion seems to have had mainly goddesses. In the mainland Greek religion, the male gods were more dynamic and powerful than their sisters and wives.

MINOAN GODDESS

MINOAN PALACE OF KNOSSOS

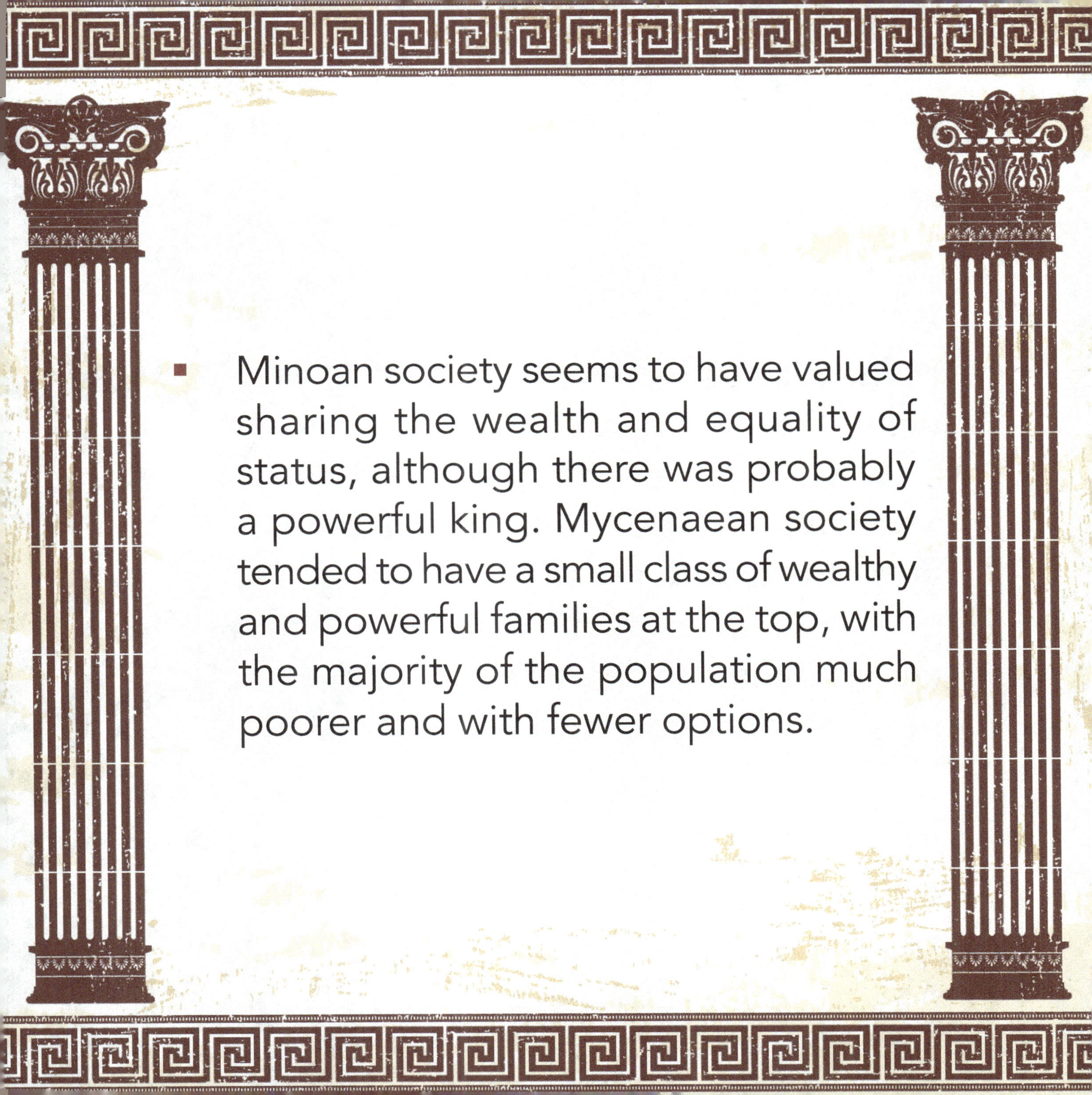

- Minoan society seems to have valued sharing the wealth and equality of status, although there was probably a powerful king. Mycenaean society tended to have a small class of wealthy and powerful families at the top, with the majority of the population much poorer and with fewer options.

- Minoan cities did not have walls. The kings and the powerful lived behind the walls of Mycenaean cities, and the poorer mass of people lived outside the walls, near the farms where they mainly worked.

RUINS OF MYCENAE, GREECE

Minoan artists were inventive and creative. Much Mycenaean art looks to be copies inspired by Minoan art.

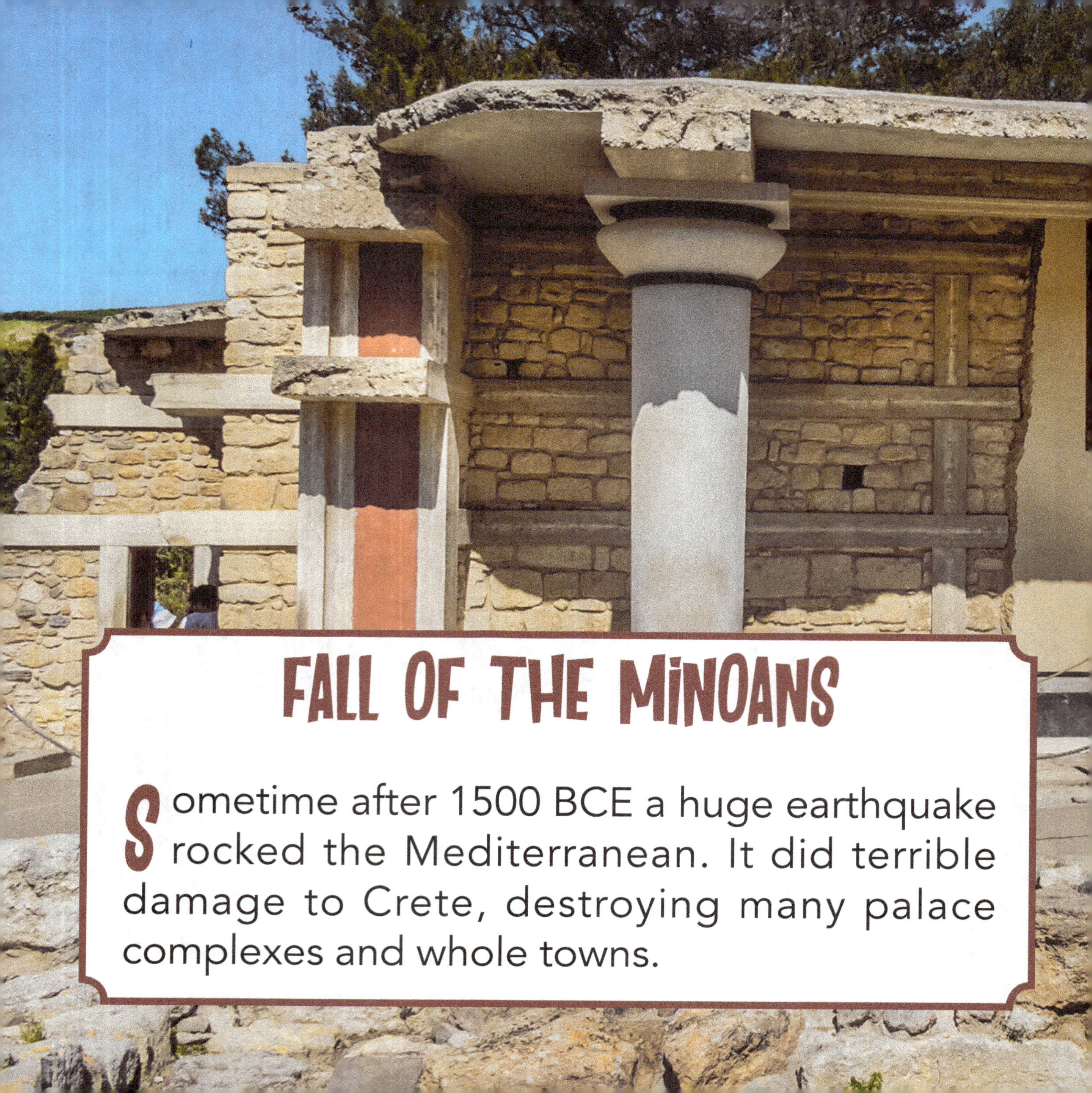

FALL OF THE MINOANS

Sometime after 1500 BCE a huge earthquake rocked the Mediterranean. It did terrible damage to Crete, destroying many palace complexes and whole towns.

RUINS OF MINOANS

CRETE, GREECE

The earthquake must also have devastated the Cretan navy and ports, because from around that time Mycenaean raiders began to attack Crete. First they came like pirates, taking whatever they could carry. Finally, around 1450 BCE, Mycenaeans invaded and conquered Crete.

he new rulers were impressed by Minoan civilization, and adopted much of it. In particular, they adapted the Linear A writing system into something we know of as Linear B for Mycenaean record-keeping. We can't read Linear B yet, either, unfortunately!

On the other hand, the Mycenaeans imposed on Crete their ideal of a militaristic, ruler-heavy society in which women did not play an active role.

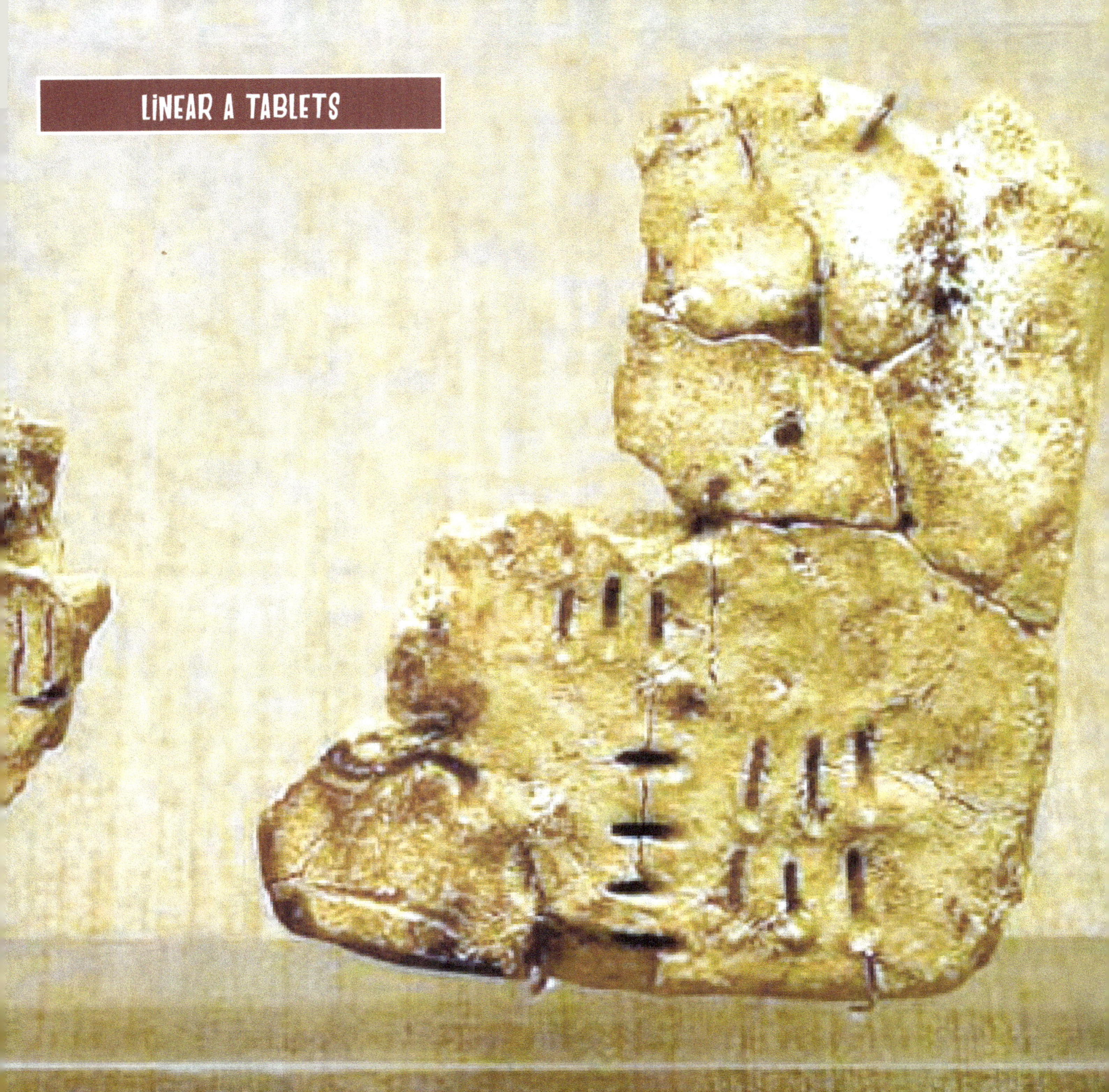

LINEAR A TABLETS

DORIAN TEMPLE

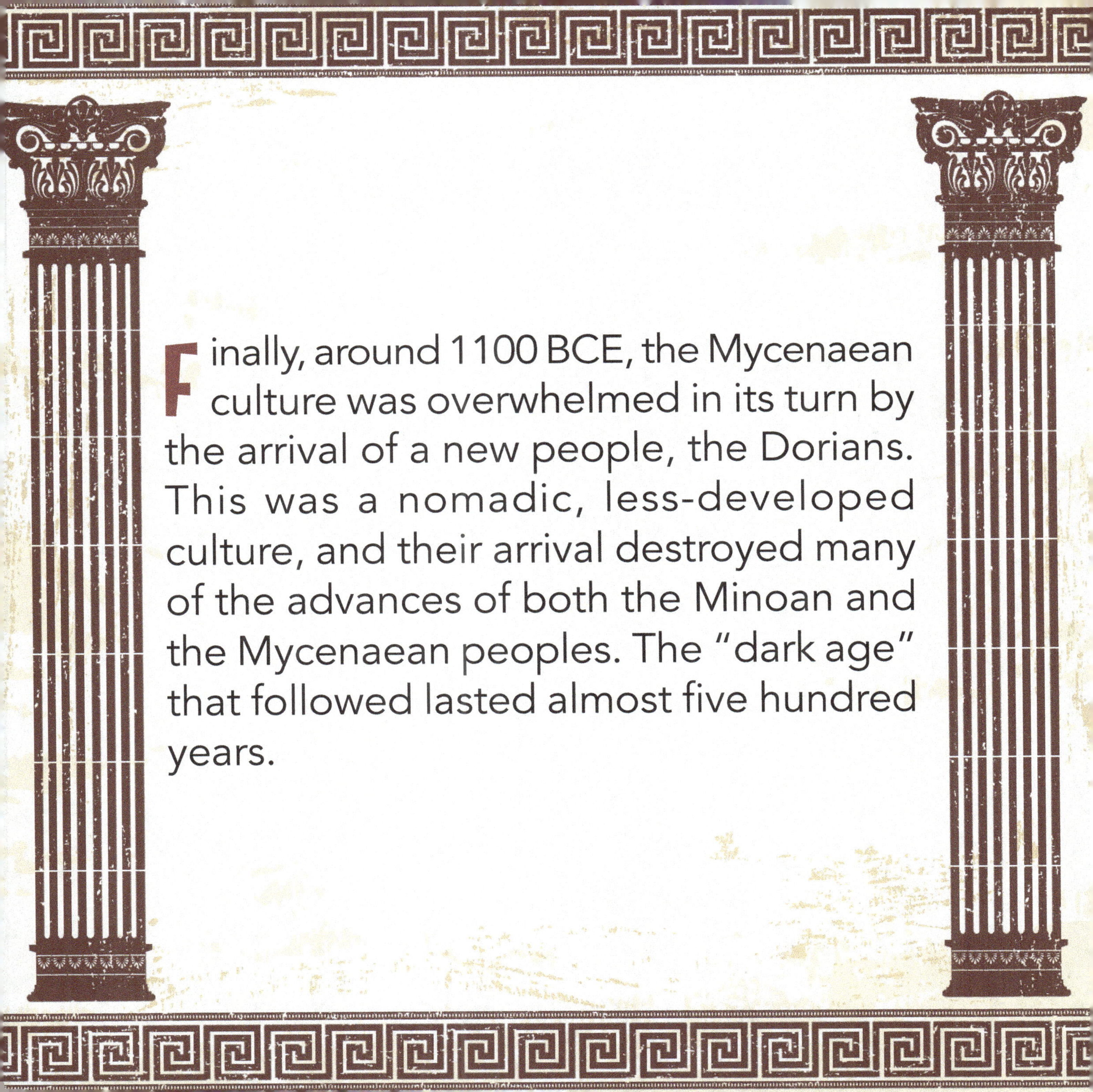

Finally, around 1100 BCE, the Mycenaean culture was overwhelmed in its turn by the arrival of a new people, the Dorians. This was a nomadic, less-developed culture, and their arrival destroyed many of the advances of both the Minoan and the Mycenaean peoples. The "dark age" that followed lasted almost five hundred years.

BLEND OR BREAK?

When two cultures collide, sometimes the stronger culture takes on many qualities of the weaker culture. Other times, the stronger culture destroys as much as it can of the weaker culture, both its people and its achievements.

To see how this has played out with other peoples, read Baby Professor books like *First Came the Sumerians Then the Akkadians, Kublai Khan: China's Mongol Emperor,* and *The Spanish Conquistadors Conquer the Aztecs.*

Visit
BABY PROFESSOR
EDUCATION KIDS
www.BabyProfessorBooks.com
to download Free Baby Professor eBooks
and view our catalog of new and exciting
Children's Books